Happy Trails,

Happy Trails,

A is for

An
Alphabet
Book

ALASKA

photography by
Daryl Pederson

text by
Amara Pederson

Publication Since 1978 Consultants

PO Box 221974 Anchorage, Alaska 99522-1974
books@publicationconsultants.com — www.publicationconsultants.com

ISBN 978-1-59433-302-6
eBook ISBN 978-1-59433-303-3
Library of Congress Catalog Card Number: 2012936968

Manufactured in the United States

I dedicate A is for Alaska to my mother for teaching me to read and write spending a lot of time homeschooling me.
        Amara

I thank my mother for buying a camera for my high school graduation gift. A perfect present from a perfect mother. I Love you Mom. Also, thank you to my cousin Karla, for challenging me.
        Daryl

A is for Alaska. The 49th state is the largest of all United States.

B is for bear. Alaska has three types of bears: Polar, Brown, and Black.

C is for caribou. Some caribou migrate thousands of miles per year.

D is for Denali. Denali is the highest mountain in North America, standing 20,320 feet tall.

E is for eagle. Alaska's eagles may weigh up to 17 pounds and have a wingspan of nearly eight feet.

F is for forget-me-not, the Alaska state flower.

G is for glacier. Alaska is home to more than 100,000 glaciers.

His for halibut. Halibut are the largest of all flat fish. Homer, Alaska is the halibut fishing capitol of the world.

I is for Iditarod. The Iditarod is 1,049 miles long. It starts in Anchorage and ends in Nome.

J is for Juneau, the Alaska state capitol.

K is for king salmon.
Kenai River is home
to a record-setting
97 pound king salmon.

L is for lupine, one of Alaska's prettiest plants. It blooms in summer with blue flowers.

M is for moose. Moose are herbivores, so they only eat plants. They can eat 40-60 pounds of food a day. Some bull moose weigh more than 1,600 pounds!

N is for northern lights. Storms on the sun make the northern night sky colorful and bright.

O is for Orca. Orcas live in family groups called pods. Male Orcas can be more than 20 feet long and weigh in excess of 12,000 pounds.

P is for puffin. These seabirds with colorful beaks make their nest in underground burrows.

Q is for qiviut. Qiviut is wool coming from the coat of the musk ox. It is known for its softness and warmth.

R is for raven. The raven is the largest member of the crow family. Ravens are considered one of the smartest birds.

S is for sea lion. The lifespan of a sea lion is around 20 years. The average size of a male sea lion is nine feet and 1,500 pounds.

T is for totem pole. Most totem poles are along the Inside Passage, in towns like Sitka and Ketchikan.

U is for ulu. An ulu is a Native women's knife used for skinning, cut-ting, eating and sewing.

V is for volcano. Alaska has more than 130 volcanoes.

W is for walrus. Their tusks can grow up to four feet long for males and two feet long for females. Walrus can live to 40 years and weigh up to 3,500 pounds.

X is for X marks the spot on the gold miners map.

Y is for Yukon.
Yukon means
the Great River.
It is more than 2,000
miles long and runs from
Canada across Alaska.

Z is for zero, a temperature often happening during Alaska winters.

Alaska Fun Facts

Alaska means the great land.

Alaska officially became the 49th state on January 3, 1959.

Alaska state flag has a blue background with eight gold stars.

Alaska has three million lakes.

Alaska state bird is the willow ptarmigan.

Alaska state gem is jade.

The largest Alaska city is Anchorage.

Lake Iliamna is 1,000 square miles.

More than half the world's active glaciers are in Alaska.

About five percent of Alaska is covered by glacier.

Alaska is 1/5 the size of the lower 48.

Alaska is larger than the next three biggest states combined.

Alaska is more than twice the size of Texas and 488 times larger than Rhode Island.

Barrow is the northernmost point in the United States.

In Barrow, the sun doesn't set for 85 days in the summer and doesn't rise for 67 days in winter.

Some halibut are bigger than my dad.

Alaska has the world's second biggest high tide, 37 feet.

Most of America's seafood comes from Alaska.

Seventeen of the twenty highest peaks in the U.S. are in Alaska.

The words to the song Alaska's Flag were written by Marie Drake, The Territorial Legislature adopted Alaska's Flag as Alaska's official song in 1955. Benny Benson described his design of the flag: The blue field is for the Alaska sky and the forget-me-not, an Alaska flower. The north star is for the future of Alaska, the most northerly in the union. The dipper is for the great bear—symbolizing strength.

Alaska State Song

Eight stars of gold on a field of blue -
Alaska's flag. May it mean to you
The blue of the sea, the evening sky,
The mountain lakes, and the flow'rs nearby;
The gold of the early sourdough's dreams,
The precious gold of the hills and streams;
The brilliant stars in the northern sky,
The "Bear" - the "Dipper" - and, shining high,
The great North Star with its steady light,
Over land and sea a beacon bright.
Alaska's flag - to Alaskans dear,
The simple flag of a last frontier.

Daryl Pederson's nature and wildlife photographs can be seen in publications such as **National Geographic, Mutual of Omahas Wild Kingdom** to name a few. He's the author of **Northern Lights, the Science, Myth and Wonder of the Aurora Borealis.**

For more information and images, go to:
www.Alaskalight.com

Amara Pederson is a lifelong Alaskan from the ski resort community of Girdwood. She enjoys fishing, skiing, swimming, soccer and volleyball.

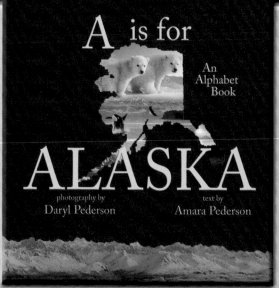

A is for

An Alphabet Book

ALASKA

photography by
Daryl Pederson

text by
Amara Pederson

To contact Daryl or Amara for book signings or to arrange
for them to be a guest speaker for your group, call or email:
Phone: (907) 563-8072 ••• dandmphoto@gmail.com

- -

Use this Coupon to Order Additional Copies

Please ship to:

First Name _____ Last Name _____

Address _____

City _____ State _____ Zip _____

Phone Number _____ email _____

		Quantity	Total
A is for Alaska	$14.95 each	_____	$ _____
Shipping and Handling	3.00 each		$ _____
No S and H with purchase of two books or more.	**Grand Total**		$ _____

Orders shipped via Air Mail the day they are received.

Credit Card Number _____ ❑ VISA

Expiration Date _____ Signature _____ ❑ MC

Publication Consultants

MasterCard 8370 Eleusis Drive, Anchorage, Alaska 99502 VISA
phone: (907) 349-2424 • fax: (907) 349-2426
www.publicationconsultants.com — email: books@publicationconsultants.com